K. CONNORS

Starting Up a Small Business

A Comprehensive Guide to Entrepreneurial Success

Copyright © 2024 by K. Connors

All rights reserved. No part of this publication may be reproduced, stored or transmitted in any form or by any means, electronic, mechanical, photocopying, recording, scanning, or otherwise without written permission from the publisher. It is illegal to copy this book, post it to a website, or distribute it by any other means without permission.

First edition

This book was professionally typeset on Reedsy.
Find out more at reedsy.com

Contents

Chapter 1: Introduction to Small Business Entrepreneurship   1
Chapter 2: Finding Your Business Idea   6
Chapter 3: Conducting Market Research   11
Chapter 4: Creating a Solid Business Plan   16
Chapter 5: Securing Funding and Managing Finances   22
Chapter 6: Legal Considerations and Business Structure   28
Chapter 7: Building Your Brand and Marketing Strategy   34
Chapter 8: Setting Up Operations and Infrastructure   41
Chapter 9: Hiring and Managing Your Team   47
Chapter 10: Scaling and Growing Your Business   52
Conclusion: Embracing the Entrepreneurial Journey   58

Chapter 1: Introduction to Small Business Entrepreneurship

Welcome to the exciting world of small business entrepreneurship! If you're reading this, chances are you've got a spark of an idea and a dream to see it flourish. Or maybe you're just tired of your 9-to-5 and ready to be your own boss. Either way, you've come to the right place. This book is your guide to navigating the thrilling, sometimes bumpy, but ultimately rewarding journey of starting your own small business.

So, why small businesses? Well, they are the backbone of our economy. Think of them as the sturdy little ants that keep the anthill running smoothly. Small businesses create jobs, foster innovation, and contribute to the local community. In fact, some of the world's biggest companies started as small ventures in a garage or a basement. Ever heard of Apple or Amazon? Yep, they started small too.

But let's not get ahead of ourselves. First things first – what does it mean to be an entrepreneur? At its core, entrepreneurship is about taking risks to create something new. It's about seeing opportunities where others see obstacles and having the grit to pursue your vision. It's not always glamorous – expect long hours, sleepless nights, and a fair share of "what-the-heck-am-I-doing" moments. But it's also incredibly fulfilling.

Now, let's break down what we'll cover in this book. We'll walk you through everything you need to know to get your business off the ground. From brainstorming your big idea to conducting market research, crafting a killer business plan, and navigating the maze of legal and financial requirements. We'll also dive into the nitty-gritty of branding, marketing, and scaling your business once you've got it up and running.

Picture this: you've got an idea for a unique coffee shop – one that not only serves amazing brews but also hosts local art and music events. It's a place where the community can gather, share stories, and enjoy great coffee. Sounds awesome, right? But where do you start? How do you know if there's a market for it? What's the best way to attract customers and keep them coming back? These are the kinds of questions we'll help you answer.

Throughout the book, we'll share real-life scenarios from successful entrepreneurs who've been in your shoes. For instance, meet Sarah, who started a boutique bakery from her home kitchen. She'll tell you about her early challenges, like that time she accidentally burned a batch of cookies for a big order (oops!). Or Alex, who turned his hobby of crafting handmade leather goods into a thriving online business. Their stories will give you a peek into the highs and lows of the entrepreneurial journey and, more importantly, the valuable lessons they learned along the way.

To kick things off, let's establish some goals for your entrepreneurial journey. Why do you want to start a business? Is it for financial independence, creative freedom, or to make a positive impact in your community? Understanding your "why" will keep you motivated when the going gets tough. Write it down, stick it on your fridge, or make it your phone wallpaper – whatever keeps that fire burning.

Here's a little exercise to get you started: Begin with a simple brainstorming session. Jot down three business ideas that excite you. They don't have to be perfect or even feasible at this stage. The goal is to get your creative juices

CHAPTER 1: INTRODUCTION TO SMALL BUSINESS ENTREPRENEURSHIP

flowing and start thinking like an entrepreneur. Remember, every big business started with a simple idea.

Let's look at the bigger picture – the role of small businesses in the economy. According to the U.S. Small Business Administration (SBA), small businesses account for 99.9% of all U.S. businesses. They employ nearly half of the private workforce and are responsible for creating two-thirds of new jobs. Small businesses are the driving force behind innovation and competition, pushing larger companies to improve and adapt. Without small businesses, our economy would lack the diversity and dynamism that makes it so robust.

Now, you might be wondering, "What makes small business owners tick?" The answer is a combination of passion, resilience, and a dash of stubbornness. Entrepreneurs are a unique breed. They see the world differently, always looking for ways to improve things, solve problems, and make an impact. They're not afraid to fail because they know failure is just a stepping stone to success. And most importantly, they believe in their vision even when others don't.

Take, for example, the story of John, who started a local organic farm. John was passionate about sustainable agriculture and wanted to provide his community with fresh, locally-grown produce. He faced numerous challenges, from unpredictable weather to market competition. But John's passion for his work kept him going. He found innovative ways to market his produce, like starting a CSA (Community Supported Agriculture) program where customers could subscribe to weekly vegetable boxes. Today, John's farm is thriving, and he's even expanded to offer farm tours and workshops on sustainable farming practices.

Another key aspect of entrepreneurship is adaptability. The business landscape is constantly changing, and successful entrepreneurs know how to pivot when necessary. Look at Jessica, who opened a small yoga studio. When the COVID-19 pandemic hit, she had to close her studio temporarily. Instead of panicking, Jessica quickly adapted by offering online classes. She invested in a good camera, learned how to use video conferencing software, and marketed her online classes through social media. Her quick thinking not only kept her business afloat but also expanded her reach to customers beyond her local area.

So, what's the secret sauce to entrepreneurial success? It's a mix of hard work, smart planning, and a bit of luck. You need a solid business plan, a clear understanding of your market, and the ability to manage your finances effectively. You also need to build a strong brand, provide excellent customer service, and continuously innovate to stay ahead of the competition.

Here are some takeaways to help you on your journey:

1. Know Your "Why": Clearly define why you want to start a business. This will keep you motivated during tough times.
   2. Start Small, Think Big: Don't be afraid to start with a small, manageable project. You can always scale up later.
   3. Learn Continuously: The business world is constantly evolving. Stay updated with industry trends and continuously improve your skills.
   4. Network: Build a strong network of mentors, peers, and industry contacts. They can provide valuable advice, support, and opportunities.
   5. Be Resilient: Entrepreneurship is a rollercoaster ride with ups and downs. Stay resilient and keep pushing forward.

In the following chapters, we'll dive deeper into each aspect of starting and running a small business. We'll provide practical advice, real-life examples, and actionable steps you can take to turn your entrepreneurial dreams into reality. So buckle up, future business owner! With a dash of creativity, a pinch of perseverance, and a healthy dose of hard work, you're on your way to making your entrepreneurial dreams a reality. Ready to dive in? Let's do this!

And remember, even the longest journey begins with a single step. So take

CHAPTER 1: INTRODUCTION TO SMALL BUSINESS ENTREPRENEURSHIP

that step today. Start with your three business ideas, and let's embark on this adventure together.

Chapter 2: Finding Your Business Idea

Alright, so you're pumped about starting a small business. Awesome! But now comes the million-dollar question: What exactly should your business be? Finding the right business idea is like finding the perfect pair of jeans – it should fit you just right, be comfortable, and ideally, look good too. Let's dive into the fun and sometimes frustrating process of discovering your golden business idea.

First things first, inspiration is everywhere. Seriously, ideas are like popcorn at a movie theater – popping up all over the place if you're paying attention. Start by looking around your daily life. What problems do you face that you wish someone would solve? What products or services do you love, but feel could be improved? Pay attention to those "I wish" moments. "I wish there was a coffee shop that offered keto-friendly pastries." "I wish there was an app that helped me find dog-friendly hiking trails." These little wishes can often spark big ideas.

Next, consider your passions and interests. What do you love to do in your free time? What topics could you talk about for hours without getting bored? Combining passion with business can be a powerful motivator. Imagine waking up every day excited about what you do – that's the dream! If you love baking, maybe a bakery is your calling. If you're a fitness enthusiast, perhaps a personal training service or a gym could be your path. The goal is to find something you're genuinely excited about because that enthusiasm will keep you going through the tough times.

Another great source of ideas is to look at what's trending. Trends are like waves – if you catch one at the right time, it can carry you a long way. Spend some time researching market trends. This doesn't mean hopping on every bandwagon, but understanding what's gaining traction can provide valuable insights. For instance, sustainability is a big trend. People are becoming more eco-conscious and looking for green alternatives. Could you offer a product or service that's environmentally friendly? Maybe a zero-waste grocery store or a line of biodegradable cleaning products?

Now, let's talk about brainstorming. Brainstorming is like a creative workout for your brain. Grab a notebook or a whiteboard, and start jotting down every idea that comes to mind. No idea is too silly or too wild at this stage. The goal is to get your creative juices flowing without judgment. Once you've got a good list, start narrowing it down. Which ideas excite you the most? Which ones align with your skills and experience? Which ones have the most potential in the market? This process helps you sift through the noise and find the gems.

Speaking of skills and experience, let's not forget to consider what you're good at. Your strengths can give you a competitive edge. If you've got a background in graphic design, maybe a design studio or a print-on-demand business could be a great fit. If you're a whiz at social media, offering consulting services to help other businesses boost their online presence could be your thing. Leveraging your skills can make the startup process smoother and increase your chances of success.

Now, let's address the elephant in the room – the fear of failure. It's totally normal to worry about whether your idea will succeed or flop. But remember, every successful entrepreneur has faced this fear. The key is to not let it paralyze you. Instead, use it as fuel to prepare and plan. Conducting thorough research and feasibility studies can help mitigate risks. Talk to potential customers, seek feedback, and refine your idea. Failure is not the end; it's a learning opportunity. Many entrepreneurs pivot and tweak their ideas before hitting the jackpot.

Here's a little exercise for you: think of three problems you've faced recently. Write them down and brainstorm possible solutions. For example, "Problem: I hate waiting in long lines at the coffee shop. Solution: A mobile app for pre-ordering and picking up your coffee." This exercise can help you start thinking like an entrepreneur and uncover potential business ideas.

Let's look at some real-life scenarios for inspiration. Meet Lisa, who loved gardening but was frustrated by the lack of organic and eco-friendly gardening supplies in her area. She saw an opportunity and started an online store selling organic seeds, compost, and eco-friendly tools. Her business not only filled a market gap but also aligned with her passion for sustainable living. Today, Lisa's store is thriving, and she's even expanded to offer virtual gardening workshops.

Then there's Tom, a tech enthusiast who noticed that many small businesses struggled with managing their online presence. He decided to start a digital marketing agency specializing in helping small businesses build and maintain their websites, manage social media, and run online ads. Tom's tech skills and understanding of the small business landscape made his agency a hit, and he's been able to help countless businesses grow their online footprint.

Another source of inspiration can be found in your own community. Pay attention to local businesses and think about what's missing. Is there a service that's lacking? A product that's in demand but hard to find? Sometimes the best ideas are right under your nose. For instance, if you live in a neighborhood with a lot of young families but no good daycare options, that could be a business opportunity. Or if you notice a lot of pet owners but no pet grooming services nearby, there's another potential idea.

Once you've honed in on a few ideas, it's time to evaluate their feasibility. This involves a bit of research and critical thinking. Ask yourself these questions: Is there a market for this product or service? Who are your potential customers? How will you reach them? What are the startup costs and potential profits? What are the challenges and risks? This step is crucial in determining whether your idea is worth pursuing.

Let's not forget about the competition. Knowing who you're up against can provide valuable insights and help you carve out your unique selling proposition (USP). Visit competitors' websites, read reviews, and understand what they're doing well and where they're falling short. This knowledge can help you differentiate your business and offer something unique.

Here's another exercise for you: pick one of your business ideas and do a quick SWOT analysis – identify the Strengths, Weaknesses, Opportunities, and Threats related to your idea. For example, if you're thinking of starting a home cleaning service, a strength might be your attention to detail, a weakness could be lack of experience in the cleaning industry, an opportunity might be the growing demand for eco-friendly cleaning services, and a threat could be established competitors. This analysis can help you get a clearer picture of what you're up against and where you can excel.

Finally, don't forget to have fun with this process. Finding your business idea should be an exciting journey of discovery. Keep an open mind, stay curious, and don't be afraid to think outside the box. The best ideas often come from the most unexpected places.

To wrap things up, here are some key takeaways to help you find your business idea:

1. Look for everyday problems that need solving. Your next big idea could be hiding in plain sight.
2. Consider your passions and interests. Building a business around something you love can be incredibly rewarding.

3. Stay informed about market trends. Understanding what's hot can help you tap into emerging opportunities.

4. Brainstorm without judgment. Let your creativity run wild and then refine your ideas.

5. Leverage your skills and experience. Your strengths can give you a competitive edge.

6. Embrace failure as a learning opportunity. Don't let fear stop you from pursuing your dreams.

7. Conduct feasibility studies. Make sure your idea has market potential and is financially viable.

8. Analyze your competition. Learn from their successes and failures to differentiate your business.

9. Do a SWOT analysis. Understand the strengths, weaknesses, opportunities, and threats related to your idea.

10. Have fun! The journey to finding your business idea should be enjoyable and inspiring.

Now that you've got a toolkit for discovering your perfect business idea, it's time to roll up your sleeves and get to work. Remember, every great business started with a simple idea and a lot of passion. So go out there, explore, and let your entrepreneurial spirit shine. Good luck!

Chapter 3: Conducting Market Research

So, you've got your big idea, and you're all set to take the entrepreneurial world by storm. But hold on a second. Before you dive in headfirst, it's crucial to understand the landscape you're about to enter. This is where market research comes in. Think of it as your business's GPS, guiding you through the twists and turns of the market to ensure you don't end up lost in a sea of competitors or stuck in a dead-end alley.

Market research is like detective work. You need to gather clues about your potential customers, understand their needs, and figure out how your business can meet those needs better than anyone else. It sounds a bit daunting, but don't worry. With a bit of effort and the right tools, you'll be able to uncover valuable insights that can set your business up for success.

Let's start with the basics. Market research can be divided into two main types: primary research and secondary research. Primary research involves collecting data directly from your target audience. It's like getting the scoop straight from the horse's mouth. This can include surveys, interviews, focus groups, and observations. On the other hand, secondary research involves gathering existing data from various sources like industry reports, academic journals, and online databases. It's like being a sponge and soaking up all the information that's already out there.

Now, you might be thinking, "Do I really need to do both?" The answer is yes. Combining primary and secondary research gives you a comprehensive understanding of the market, allowing you to make informed decisions. It's like building a puzzle; you need all the pieces to see the complete picture.

Let's talk about primary research first. One of the most common methods is surveys. Surveys are a great way to gather quantitative data from a large group of people. You can use online survey tools like SurveyMonkey or Google Forms to create and distribute your survey. When designing your survey, keep it short and sweet. No one likes a never-ending questionnaire. Ask clear, concise questions and avoid leading questions that might bias the responses. For example, instead of asking, "Don't you think our product is amazing?" ask, "How would you rate our product on a scale of 1 to 10?"

Interviews and focus groups, on the other hand, are more qualitative. They allow you to dive deeper into people's thoughts and feelings. Interviews can be conducted one-on-one, either in person or over the phone. They provide an opportunity to ask open-ended questions and follow up on interesting points. Focus groups involve bringing together a small group of people to discuss a specific topic. It's like a roundtable discussion where participants can bounce ideas off each other. These methods can provide rich, detailed insights that surveys might miss.

Observation is another useful primary research method. This involves watching how people interact with products or services in real-world settings. For example, if you're opening a retail store, you might spend some time observing shoppers in similar stores. Pay attention to what catches their eye, how they navigate the space, and what products they pick up and put back. This can give you valuable insights into customer behavior and preferences.

Now, let's move on to secondary research. This involves collecting and analyzing existing data from various sources. Start by looking at industry reports from reputable sources like IBISWorld or Statista. These reports can provide a wealth of information about market size, trends, and competitive landscape.

CHAPTER 3: CONDUCTING MARKET RESEARCH

Government publications and trade associations are also valuable sources of data. For example, the U.S. Census Bureau provides data on population demographics, which can help you understand your target audience.

Academic journals and research papers can also be useful, especially if you're entering a specialized field. Online databases like JSTOR or Google Scholar can help you find relevant studies. Additionally, don't underestimate the power of a good old-fashioned Google search. There are countless articles, blogs, and forums where you can gather insights about your industry.

Social media is another goldmine of information. Platforms like Facebook, Twitter, and Instagram allow you to see what people are talking about in real-time. Look for groups or communities related to your industry and pay attention to the discussions. What are people complaining about? What are they excited about? This can give you a sense of the current trends and issues.

Once you've gathered all this data, it's time to analyze it. Look for patterns and trends that can inform your business strategy. For example, if your research shows that there's a growing demand for eco-friendly products, you might decide to focus on sustainability as a key selling point for your business. If you discover that your target audience values convenience, you might prioritize creating a seamless online shopping experience.

Let's look at a real-life scenario. Meet Dave, who wanted to open a food truck serving gourmet grilled cheese sandwiches. Dave had a great product, but he wasn't sure where to set up shop or how to attract customers. So, he decided to do some market research. Dave started with primary research, conducting surveys at local events to gauge people's interest in gourmet grilled cheese. He asked questions like, "How often do you eat at food trucks?" and "What flavors of grilled cheese would you like to see?"

Next, Dave held a few focus groups with potential customers to get more detailed feedback. He brought samples of his sandwiches and asked participants to rate them and provide suggestions for improvement. He also observed other food trucks in action, noting their busiest locations and popular menu items.

For secondary research, Dave looked at industry reports on the food truck market. He discovered that food trucks were becoming increasingly popular, especially in urban areas. He also found data on the most profitable locations and peak times for food truck business. Dave even scoured social media to see what people were saying about food trucks in his city.

Armed with this information, Dave was able to make informed decisions. He chose a busy downtown location for his food truck, developed a menu based on customer preferences, and marketed his business through social media, highlighting the gourmet and unique aspects of his grilled cheese sandwiches. His market research paid off, and Dave's food truck became a hit.

To wrap up this chapter, here are some key takeaways for conducting market research:

1. Use a combination of primary and secondary research to get a complete picture of the market.
2. Design surveys that are clear and concise, avoiding leading questions.
3. Conduct interviews and focus groups to gather detailed, qualitative insights.
4. Observe customer behavior in real-world settings to understand their preferences.
5. Gather data from reputable sources like industry reports, government publications, and academic journals.
6. Leverage social media to stay up-to-date with trends and customer sentiment.
7. Analyze the data to identify patterns and trends that can inform your business strategy.
8. Be prepared to adapt your business idea based on your findings.

CHAPTER 3: CONDUCTING MARKET RESEARCH

Market research might not be the most glamorous part of starting a business, but it's definitely one of the most important. It helps you understand your customers, identify opportunities, and avoid potential pitfalls. So, put on your detective hat, grab your magnifying glass, and start uncovering the insights that will guide your business to success. Happy researching!

Chapter 4: Creating a Solid Business Plan

Congratulations, intrepid entrepreneur! You've come up with a fantastic business idea, and you've done your homework with market research. Now, it's time to build the blueprint for your business empire: the business plan. Think of it as the detailed map that will guide you on your journey from startup to success. A well-crafted business plan not only helps you clarify your vision but also shows potential investors and partners that you're serious about making your idea a reality.

First things first, let's demystify what a business plan actually is. Essentially, it's a formal document that outlines your business goals, the strategy for achieving them, and the timeline for implementation. It's like a master plan that answers all the crucial questions about your business: what, why, who, where, and how. This might sound a bit overwhelming, but don't worry—we'll break it down into manageable chunks.

Your business plan should start with an executive summary. This is a brief overview of your business and your plan. Think of it as your business's elevator pitch. It should be engaging, concise, and compelling enough to make readers want to dive into the rest of your plan. The executive summary should cover the basics: your business idea, your mission statement, and a brief description of your products or services. You should also include a snapshot of your financial projections and your funding requirements if you're seeking investment.

CHAPTER 4: CREATING A SOLID BUSINESS PLAN

Next up is the company description. This section provides more detailed information about your business. What problem are you solving? What makes your business unique? Describe your target market and how you plan to serve them. This is also where you'll outline your business structure. Are you a sole proprietor, a partnership, an LLC, or a corporation? Each structure has its own legal and tax implications, so choose wisely.

Let's move on to the market analysis. This is where all that market research you did earlier comes into play. You need to demonstrate that there's a demand for your product or service and that you understand your industry and your competitors. Start by describing your industry's current landscape and future outlook. Include data on market size, growth trends, and regulatory environment. Then, dive into your target market. Who are your customers? What are their needs and preferences? How big is your target market, and what is its growth potential? Finally, analyze your competitors. Who are they, and what are their strengths and weaknesses? How will you differentiate your business from theirs?

The next section of your business plan is the organization and management structure. Here, you'll outline your business's organizational structure and introduce your team. This includes the owners, the management team, and any key employees. Provide brief bios highlighting their experience and qualifications. If you have an advisory board or any external consultants, mention them here too. Investors want to know that your business is in capable hands, so showcase your team's expertise and what makes them the right people to execute your vision.

Now, let's talk about your products or services. This section should provide a detailed description of what you're offering. What are the features and benefits of your products or services? How do they meet the needs of your target market? If you have any patents, trademarks, or proprietary technology, mention them here. Also, outline your product development or production process. How will you source materials, manufacture your products, or deliver your services? Provide a roadmap for any future product development or service enhancements.

Next up is the marketing and sales strategy. This is where you'll detail how you plan to attract and retain customers. Start with your marketing strategy. What's your brand identity, and how will you position yourself in the market? Outline your pricing strategy, distribution channels, and promotional tactics. How will you use advertising, social media, content marketing, or public relations to reach your target audience? Then, move on to your sales strategy. What's your sales process, and how will you convert leads into customers? Do you have a sales team, and if so, what's their structure and compensation plan? The goal is to show that you have a clear and actionable plan for growing your customer base.

The financial plan and projections section is next, and it's a biggie. This is where you'll present your financial forecasts and funding requirements. Investors will scrutinize this section, so it needs to be thorough and realistic. Start with your revenue model. How will your business make money? What are your main revenue streams? Then, provide your financial projections for the next three to five years. This should include income statements, cash flow statements, and balance sheets. Be sure to explain the assumptions behind your projections. If you're seeking funding, outline how much you need, what you'll use it for, and how you plan to repay it or provide a return on investment.

Finally, include an appendix. This section isn't always necessary, but it can be useful for including supplementary information that supports your business plan. This could be market research data, detailed financial projections, legal documents, product photos, or anything else that adds value to your plan.

Let's look at a real-life example. Meet Rachel, who wants to start a handmade jewelry business. Here's how she approached her business plan:

Rachel's executive summary started with a bang. She described her vision for

CHAPTER 4: CREATING A SOLID BUSINESS PLAN

unique, eco-friendly jewelry that combines modern design with traditional craftsmanship. She highlighted her mission to provide customers with high-quality, sustainable products while supporting local artisans.

In her company description, Rachel detailed the problem she was solving: the lack of stylish, eco-friendly jewelry options. She explained how her business would stand out by using recycled materials and partnering with local artisans. She outlined her target market: environmentally conscious consumers who value unique, handcrafted products. Rachel also described her business structure as an LLC to protect her personal assets.

For her market analysis, Rachel conducted extensive research on the jewelry industry. She found that the market for eco-friendly products was growing rapidly. She identified her target customers as women aged 25-45 with disposable income and a commitment to sustainability. Rachel also analyzed her competitors, noting their strengths in marketing but weaknesses in product sustainability and uniqueness.

In the organization and management section, Rachel introduced herself as the founder and head designer, highlighting her background in fashion design and business. She also mentioned her advisory board, which included a marketing expert and a financial advisor, to show she had a strong support system.

Rachel's products and services section was a detailed showcase of her jewelry line. She described the features and benefits of her pieces, such as the use of recycled silver and unique, hand-crafted designs. She outlined her production process, from sourcing materials to working with local artisans to create her jewelry.

In her marketing and sales strategy, Rachel laid out her brand identity as a blend of modern and traditional, with a focus on sustainability. She planned to sell her products through an online store, at artisan markets, and through select boutique retailers. Rachel's promotional tactics included social media marketing, influencer partnerships, and eco-friendly packaging to reinforce her brand values. She also detailed her sales process, emphasizing excellent customer service and a seamless online shopping experience.

For her financial plan and projections, Rachel presented a detailed revenue model based on sales of her jewelry. She provided income statements, cash flow statements, and balance sheets, showing a clear path to profitability. Rachel explained her funding requirements, specifying that she needed $50,000 to cover initial production costs, marketing, and website development. She outlined how she planned to use the funds and her strategy for achieving a return on investment.

In her appendix, Rachel included detailed market research data, photos of her jewelry, and testimonials from customers who had bought her initial pieces. This supplementary information added depth to her business plan and demonstrated the viability of her business idea.

Rachel's comprehensive business plan impressed investors and secured the funding she needed to launch her business. Today, her jewelry brand is thriving, and she continues to expand her product line and market reach.

As you craft your business plan, remember that it's not just a document to secure funding. It's a living, breathing guide that you'll refer to and update as your business grows. Keep it clear, concise, and focused on your goals. Use it to stay on track, make informed decisions, and adapt to changing circumstances.

Here are some key takeaways to help you create a solid business plan:

1. Start with a compelling executive summary to capture the reader's attention.
    2. Provide a detailed company description, explaining the problem you're solving and what makes your business unique.
    3. Conduct thorough market analysis to demonstrate your understanding of the industry and your target market.

4. Outline your organization and management structure, highlighting your team's expertise.

5. Describe your products or services in detail, including features, benefits, and production process.

6. Develop a comprehensive marketing and sales strategy to attract and retain customers.

7. Present realistic financial projections and funding requirements, explaining your revenue model and financial assumptions.

8. Include an appendix with supplementary information to support your business plan.

9. Remember that your business plan is a dynamic tool that should evolve with your business.

10. Use your business plan to guide your decisions and keep you focused on your goals.

Creating a solid business plan is a crucial step in turning your entrepreneurial dreams into reality. It's your roadmap to success, helping you navigate the challenges and seize the opportunities along the way. So roll up your sleeves, get writing, and let your business plan guide you to success. Happy planning!

Chapter 5: Securing Funding and Managing Finances

Alright, you've got your business idea, your market research, and your business plan all squared away. Now comes a crucial part of your entrepreneurial journey: securing funding and managing your finances. Think of this chapter as your financial boot camp. We'll cover the basics, explore different funding options, and help you set up a solid financial foundation for your business.

Let's start with the big question: how much money do you actually need to get started? This depends on your business model, industry, and growth plans. For instance, starting a home-based online store will cost significantly less than opening a brick-and-mortar restaurant. Your business plan should already have a detailed breakdown of your startup costs, but here's a quick recap. Consider expenses like equipment, inventory, licenses and permits, marketing, website development, and initial working capital.

Once you have a ballpark figure, it's time to explore your funding options. There are several ways to fund your business, and each has its pros and cons. Let's break down some of the most common options:

1. **Bootstrapping**: This is the DIY approach to funding your business using your own savings or revenue generated by the business. It's a great option if you want to maintain full control and avoid debt. However, it can be risky if

CHAPTER 5: SECURING FUNDING AND MANAGING FINANCES

your savings are limited and you don't have a steady income stream to support your business expenses.

2. **Friends and Family**: Borrowing money from friends and family can be a quick and easy way to raise funds. Just remember to keep things professional. Draft a formal agreement outlining the terms of the loan or investment to avoid any misunderstandings or strained relationships down the road. Treat it like a business transaction, because that's exactly what it is.

3. **Small Business Loans**: Banks and credit unions offer various loans specifically designed for small businesses. The Small Business Administration (SBA) in the U.S. provides loan programs that can make it easier for small businesses to get funding. The application process can be lengthy and requires a solid business plan and good credit. But the interest rates are often lower than other financing options, and you retain full ownership of your business.

4. **Investors**: This includes angel investors and venture capitalists who provide capital in exchange for equity in your business. Angel investors are usually wealthy individuals who invest their own money, while venture capitalists manage pooled funds from multiple investors. Both can provide significant funding and valuable mentorship, but you'll have to give up a portion of ownership and control. Make sure you're comfortable with this trade-off before pursuing this route.

5. **Crowdfunding**: Platforms like Kickstarter, Indiegogo, and GoFundMe allow you to raise small amounts of money from a large number of people. It's a great way to validate your business idea and build a community of early supporters. Successful crowdfunding campaigns often involve offering perks or rewards to backers, such as early access to products or exclusive merchandise. It requires a strong marketing effort, but it can be a fun and engaging way to raise funds.

6. **Grants**: While less common, grants are essentially free money

provided by government agencies, nonprofit organizations, or corporations to support specific types of businesses or initiatives. Grants typically don't need to be repaid, but they often come with stringent requirements and a competitive application process. Do some research to see if there are any grants available for your industry or business type.

Whichever funding option you choose, it's crucial to manage your finances wisely. Here are some tips to help you stay on top of your financial game:

1. **Create a Budget**: A detailed budget is your financial roadmap. It helps you track your income and expenses, allocate funds appropriately, and avoid overspending. Break down your budget into categories like rent, utilities, marketing, salaries, and inventory. Review and update it regularly to reflect changes in your business.

2. **Keep Personal and Business Finances Separate**: Open a dedicated business bank account and get a business credit card. This not only simplifies bookkeeping but also helps build your business credit. It's essential for maintaining a clear picture of your business's financial health and ensuring accurate tax reporting.

3. **Monitor Cash Flow**: Cash flow is the lifeblood of your business. Even profitable businesses can fail if they run out of cash. Keep a close eye on your cash flow by tracking incoming and outgoing funds. Use accounting software to generate cash flow statements and forecasts. This will help you anticipate shortfalls and take proactive measures to address them.

4. **Plan for Taxes**: Taxes are an inevitable part of running a business. Make sure you understand your tax obligations and set aside funds for tax payments. Consider working with an accountant or tax advisor to ensure compliance and take advantage of any tax deductions or credits available to your business.

CHAPTER 5: SECURING FUNDING AND MANAGING FINANCES

5. **Build an Emergency Fund**: Unexpected expenses or slow periods can put a strain on your finances. Aim to set aside a portion of your profits into an emergency fund. This financial cushion can help you navigate challenges without resorting to high-interest loans or dipping into your personal savings.

6. **Review Financial Statements Regularly**: Financial statements, including income statements, balance sheets, and cash flow statements, provide valuable insights into your business's performance. Review these statements regularly to monitor your profitability, liquidity, and overall financial health. This information will help you make informed decisions and identify areas for improvement.

7. **Control Costs**: Keeping costs under control is essential for maintaining profitability. Regularly review your expenses and look for opportunities to cut costs or improve efficiency. Negotiate with suppliers for better terms, consider outsourcing non-core tasks, and implement cost-saving measures like energy-efficient practices.

8. **Seek Professional Advice**: Don't hesitate to seek advice from financial professionals, such as accountants, bookkeepers, and financial advisors. They can provide valuable guidance on budgeting, tax planning, and financial strategy. Investing in professional advice can save you money in the long run and help you avoid costly mistakes.

Now, let's consider a real-life scenario. Meet Laura, who wants to open a boutique clothing store. Laura has a solid business plan and has identified her target market, but she needs $75,000 to cover her startup costs, including inventory, rent, and marketing. Here's how Laura approached her funding and financial management:

Laura started by evaluating her savings and decided to bootstrap part of her business. She allocated $20,000 of her savings to cover initial expenses. Next, she approached her family and friends and raised an additional $15,000 in small loans, ensuring she had formal agreements in place to avoid any future misunderstandings.

To cover the remaining $40,000, Laura applied for an SBA loan. She prepared a detailed loan application, including her business plan, financial projections, and personal financial statements. After a thorough review, she was approved for the loan with favorable terms.

With her funding secured, Laura focused on setting up her financial systems. She opened a business bank account and obtained a business credit card. She also invested in accounting software to track her income and expenses and generate financial reports.

Laura created a comprehensive budget, outlining her projected income and expenses for the first year. She included categories for rent, utilities, inventory, marketing, and salaries. By regularly reviewing and updating her budget, Laura was able to stay on track and make adjustments as needed.

To ensure she was prepared for any financial surprises, Laura built an emergency fund by setting aside a portion of her profits each month. This fund provided a safety net, allowing her to cover unexpected expenses without jeopardizing her business's financial stability.

Laura also sought the advice of a financial advisor, who helped her develop a tax strategy and identify potential cost-saving opportunities. With their guidance, she was able to maximize her tax deductions and improve her overall financial efficiency.

By taking a proactive approach to securing funding and managing her finances, Laura set her boutique clothing store up for success. She was able to navigate the challenges of entrepreneurship and build a thriving business.

In conclusion, securing funding and managing your finances are critical steps in launching and sustaining a successful business. By exploring different funding options, creating a detailed budget, and implementing sound financial practices, you can build a strong financial foundation for your business. Remember, financial management is an ongoing process, so stay vigilant, seek professional advice when needed, and always keep an eye on your cash flow.

With these strategies in place, you'll be well-equipped to handle the financial aspects of your business and focus on what you do best: bringing your entrepreneurial vision to life. So go ahead, crunch those numbers, and let your business thrive!

Chapter 6: Legal Considerations and Business Structure

Alright, future business mogul, let's get down to brass tacks. You've got the idea, you've done your research, and you've even figured out how to get your hands on some cold hard cash. Now, it's time to navigate the somewhat less glamorous but utterly essential world of legal considerations and business structure. Think of this as the sturdy foundation upon which you'll build your business empire. Neglecting this step is like trying to build a house on quicksand—not a good idea. So, let's dive in.

First things first: choosing the right business structure. This decision will affect everything from how you file your taxes to how much personal liability you face if things go south. There are several types of business structures to choose from, each with its own set of pros and cons.

Let's start with the simplest form: the sole proprietorship. If you're planning to go it alone, this might be the easiest way to get started. A sole proprietorship is a business owned and run by one person. It's super straightforward and doesn't require any formal setup. The downside? There's no legal distinction between you and your business. This means that if your business incurs debt or gets sued, your personal assets are on the line. So, while it's easy to set up, it carries a fair bit of risk.

CHAPTER 6: LEGAL CONSIDERATIONS AND BUSINESS STRUCTURE

Next up is the partnership, which is great if you're planning to start a business with one or more people. There are two main types: general partnerships and limited partnerships. In a general partnership, all partners share equal responsibility for the business and its debts. In a limited partnership, you have both general partners (who manage the business and assume liability) and limited partners (who are typically investors with limited liability). Partnerships are relatively easy to form but can get complicated if there's a falling out between partners. It's crucial to have a solid partnership agreement that outlines each partner's role, investment, and how profits and losses will be shared.

Then there's the Limited Liability Company, or LLC. This structure is popular for small businesses because it offers the best of both worlds: the liability protection of a corporation with the tax benefits and flexibility of a partnership. With an LLC, your personal assets are protected from business debts and lawsuits. Plus, you can choose how you want to be taxed—either as a sole proprietor, partnership, or corporation. Forming an LLC requires a bit more paperwork and money than a sole proprietorship or partnership, but the peace of mind it offers can be well worth it.

If you're thinking big—like, really big—a corporation might be the way to go. There are two main types: C corporations and S corporations. C corporations are the big guys you hear about all the time. They can raise money by selling stock, and they offer strong liability protection. However, they're subject to double taxation: the corporation pays taxes on its profits, and shareholders pay taxes on dividends. S corporations, on the other hand, avoid double taxation by passing income directly to shareholders, who then report it on their personal tax returns. Both types require more extensive record-keeping, operational processes, and reporting than other business structures.

Alright, now that we've covered the basics of business structures, let's move on to some other legal considerations. One of the first things you'll need to do is register your business name. This is known as your "Doing Business As"

(DBA) name. It's the name the public will know your business by, so make sure it's catchy, memorable, and, most importantly, available. Check with your local government or online databases to ensure no one else is using the name you want.

Next, you'll need to obtain the necessary licenses and permits to operate legally. This varies depending on your business type and location. For example, if you're opening a restaurant, you'll need health permits, food handler's permits, and possibly liquor licenses. If you're starting a home-based business, you might need a home occupation permit. Do your homework and make sure you're in compliance with all local, state, and federal regulations.

Taxes. Everyone's favorite topic, right? While it's not the most exciting part of running a business, it's one of the most important. First, you'll need to get an Employer Identification Number (EIN) from the IRS. Think of it as your business's social security number. You'll use it to file your taxes, open a business bank account, and apply for business licenses. The type of taxes you'll need to pay depends on your business structure. Sole proprietors and partnerships will report business income on their personal tax returns, while corporations will file separate tax returns. You might also need to pay employment taxes if you have employees, as well as state and local taxes. This is where a good accountant can be worth their weight in gold.

Another critical aspect to consider is insurance. Business insurance can protect you from various risks, including property damage, liability claims, and employee-related issues. Here are a few types of insurance to consider:

1. **General Liability Insurance**: This covers you against claims of bodily injury or property damage caused by your business operations, products, or services.

2. **Property Insurance**: If you own or lease space for your business, property insurance protects your building, equipment, inventory, and other

CHAPTER 6: LEGAL CONSIDERATIONS AND BUSINESS STRUCTURE

assets from damage or theft.

3. **Workers' Compensation Insurance**: If you have employees, workers' compensation insurance covers medical expenses and lost wages if they're injured on the job. Most states require businesses with employees to carry this insurance.

4. **Professional Liability Insurance**: Also known as errors and omissions insurance, this covers you if you're sued for negligence or mistakes in the services you provide.

5. **Product Liability Insurance**: If you manufacture or sell products, this insurance protects you against claims of injury or damage caused by your products.

6. **Business Interruption Insurance**: This covers lost income and operating expenses if your business is temporarily closed due to a covered event, such as a natural disaster.

Choosing the right insurance policies for your business can be complex, so it's a good idea to work with an insurance agent who understands your industry.

Now, let's talk about contracts. Whether you're dealing with suppliers, customers, or employees, having clear, written contracts is essential. Contracts protect your business by outlining the terms and conditions of an agreement, including payment terms, deliverables, deadlines, and responsibilities. Make sure all contracts are legally binding and reviewed by a lawyer. Verbal agreements might be easier, but they can lead to misunderstandings and disputes down the road.

Speaking of lawyers, it's wise to have legal counsel on your side. A good business lawyer can help you with everything from choosing the right business structure to drafting contracts and ensuring compliance with regulations.

While hiring a lawyer might seem like a significant expense, it can save you money in the long run by preventing legal issues and protecting your business interests.

Finally, let's touch on intellectual property (IP). If you've created something unique, such as a product, logo, or piece of content, you'll want to protect it. Here are a few ways to safeguard your IP:

1. **Trademarks**: Trademarks protect brand names, logos, and slogans. Registering a trademark gives you exclusive rights to use the mark in connection with your products or services and helps prevent others from using a similar mark.

2. **Copyrights**: Copyrights protect original works of authorship, such as books, music, art, and software. Copyright protection is automatic once the work is created, but registering it provides additional legal benefits.

3. **Patents**: Patents protect new inventions and processes. Obtaining a patent gives you the exclusive right to make, use, and sell your invention for a certain period. The patent application process can be lengthy and complex, so it's often best to work with a patent attorney.

4. **Trade Secrets**: Trade secrets are confidential business information that gives your company a competitive edge, such as formulas, processes, or customer lists. Protect trade secrets by implementing confidentiality agreements and security measures.

To illustrate the importance of legal considerations, let's look at a real-life example. Meet Mike, who wanted to start a tech consulting business. Mike had a brilliant idea and a solid business plan, but he underestimated the importance of legalities. He set up a sole proprietorship and started operating under a catchy name without checking if it was already in use. A few months later, Mike received a cease-and-desist letter from a company with a similar name,

CHAPTER 6: LEGAL CONSIDERATIONS AND BUSINESS STRUCTURE

forcing him to rebrand. He also faced a hefty fine for operating without the necessary business licenses. Mike quickly realized the importance of getting legal ducks in a row and sought the help of a lawyer to ensure compliance and protect his business.

In conclusion, while legal considerations and business structure might not be the most exciting aspects of starting a business, they are absolutely critical to your success. By choosing the right business structure, obtaining the necessary licenses and permits, understanding your tax obligations, securing appropriate insurance, and protecting your intellectual property, you'll build a solid foundation for your business.

Here are some key takeaways to help you navigate the legal landscape:

1. Choose the right business structure based on your needs and goals.
2. Register your business name and ensure it's unique.
3. Obtain the necessary licenses and permits to operate legally.
4. Get an EIN and understand your tax obligations.
5. Keep personal and business finances separate.
6. Invest in appropriate insurance to protect your business.
7. Use clear, written contracts for all business dealings.
8. Seek legal advice to ensure compliance and protect your interests.
9. Safeguard your intellectual property with trademarks, copyrights, patents, or trade secrets.
10. Stay informed about changes in laws and regulations that affect your business.

By taking care of these legal considerations, you can focus on what you do best—growing your business and

achieving your entrepreneurial dreams. So, roll up your sleeves, tackle the legal stuff, and set your business on the path to success.

Chapter 7: Building Your Brand and Marketing Strategy

Alright, it's time to get creative and a bit flashy. Building your brand and crafting a killer marketing strategy are like dressing your business in its Sunday best and making sure everyone in town knows just how fabulous it looks. Your brand is more than just a logo or a catchy tagline; it's the heart and soul of your business. It's what makes you unique, memorable, and relatable to your customers. And your marketing strategy? That's how you spread the word and attract those customers like bees to honey.

Let's start with the foundation of your brand: your brand identity. This includes your business name, logo, colors, fonts, and overall aesthetic. It's the visual and emotional representation of your business. Think of it as the personality of your brand. Are you fun and playful like Ben & Jerry's, or sleek and sophisticated like Apple? Your brand identity should reflect the essence of your business and resonate with your target audience.

Begin by defining your brand values and mission. What do you stand for? What are you passionate about? Your values and mission will guide all your branding efforts and ensure consistency. For example, if you're starting an eco-friendly clothing line, your brand values might include sustainability, ethical production, and community support. Your mission could be to provide stylish, sustainable fashion that empowers consumers to make environmentally

CHAPTER 7: BUILDING YOUR BRAND AND MARKETING STRATEGY

conscious choices.

Next, create a memorable logo. Your logo is the face of your brand and will be everywhere—on your website, social media, business cards, and products. It should be simple, versatile, and instantly recognizable. Consider working with a professional graphic designer to ensure your logo stands out and accurately represents your brand. While you're at it, choose your brand colors and fonts. These elements should complement your logo and convey the right mood and tone. For instance, bright colors and playful fonts might work well for a children's toy store, while muted tones and elegant fonts might suit a luxury spa.

Now that you've nailed down your brand identity, let's talk about your brand voice. This is how you communicate with your audience. It includes your tone, language, and overall style. Are you casual and conversational, or formal and authoritative? Your brand voice should be consistent across all your marketing channels and materials. It helps build a strong connection with your audience and reinforces your brand identity. For example, if your brand is all about fun and creativity, your social media posts, blog articles, and customer emails should reflect that with a friendly and upbeat tone.

Alright, with your brand identity and voice in place, it's time to craft your marketing strategy. This is how you'll attract, engage, and retain customers. A solid marketing strategy involves several key components, so let's break them down.

First, understand your target audience. Who are they? What are their needs, preferences, and pain points? Creating detailed buyer personas can help you get a clear picture of your ideal customers. A buyer persona is a semi-fictional representation of your target customer based on market research and real data. Include details like age, gender, occupation, income, interests, and buying behavior. Knowing your audience inside out allows you to tailor your marketing efforts to meet their specific needs and preferences.

Next, set your marketing goals. What do you want to achieve with your marketing efforts? Your goals should be specific, measurable, achievable, relevant, and time-bound (SMART). For example, instead of saying, "I want more customers," set a goal like, "I want to increase website traffic by 20% in the next three months." Having clear goals helps you stay focused and track your progress.

Once you've set your goals, choose your marketing channels. There are many ways to reach your audience, so it's important to select the channels that are most effective for your business and target audience. Here are some popular options:

1. **Social Media**: Platforms like Facebook, Instagram, Twitter, and LinkedIn are powerful tools for building brand awareness and engaging with your audience. Each platform has its own strengths and demographics, so choose the ones that align with your target audience. For example, Instagram is great for visual content and younger audiences, while LinkedIn is ideal for B2B marketing and professional networking.

2. **Content Marketing**: Creating valuable and relevant content helps attract and engage your audience. This can include blog articles, videos, podcasts, infographics, and more. Content marketing establishes you as an authority in your industry and builds trust with your audience. Focus on providing useful information that addresses your audience's needs and pain points.

3. **Email Marketing**: Email is a direct and personal way to communicate with your audience. Use it to share updates, promotions, and valuable content. Build an email list by offering incentives like discounts or exclusive content in exchange for signing up. Segment your list to send targeted and relevant emails to different groups of subscribers.

4. **Search Engine Optimization (SEO)**: SEO helps your website rank higher

CHAPTER 7: BUILDING YOUR BRAND AND MARKETING STRATEGY

in search engine results, making it easier for potential customers to find you. Optimize your website and content with relevant keywords, meta tags, and high-quality backlinks. A strong SEO strategy can drive organic traffic to your site and increase your visibility.

5. **Pay-Per-Click (PPC) Advertising**: PPC ads, such as Google Ads or social media ads, allow you to target specific keywords or demographics. You pay only when someone clicks on your ad, making it a cost-effective way to reach potential customers. PPC campaigns can generate immediate traffic and leads, but they require careful planning and monitoring to ensure a positive return on investment.

6. **Influencer Marketing**: Partnering with influencers can help you reach a broader audience and build credibility. Choose influencers who align with your brand values and have a genuine connection with their followers. Collaborations can include sponsored posts, product reviews, or social media takeovers.

7. **Public Relations (PR)**: PR involves managing your brand's image and building relationships with the media. This can include press releases, media coverage, and event sponsorships. Positive PR can boost your brand's reputation and increase awareness.

Now that you've chosen your marketing channels, it's time to create a content calendar. A content calendar helps you plan and organize your marketing activities. It ensures consistency and keeps you on track with your goals. Include important dates, such as product launches, holidays, and promotions, and schedule your content accordingly. Plan a mix of content types, like blog posts, social media updates, videos, and emails, to keep your audience engaged.

Measuring the effectiveness of your marketing efforts is crucial. Use analytics tools to track key performance indicators (KPIs) such as website traffic, social media engagement, email open rates, and conversion rates. Analyzing these metrics helps you understand what's working and what's not, so you can make data-driven decisions and optimize your strategy.

Let's look at a real-life example. Meet Emily, who wants to start a handmade candle business. Here's how she built her brand and marketing strategy:

Emily began by defining her brand identity. She chose a business name, "Cozy Glow," and worked with a designer to create a warm, inviting logo featuring a candle flame. Her brand colors were soft pastels, and her fonts were elegant and easy to read. Emily's brand values included sustainability, quality, and comfort, and her mission was to create eco-friendly candles that bring a sense of coziness to any space.

Emily developed a friendly and conversational brand voice, which she used consistently across all her marketing channels. She created buyer personas for her target audience, which included busy professionals looking to relax, environmentally conscious consumers, and gift shoppers seeking unique, handmade products.

Emily set her marketing goals, such as increasing her Instagram followers by 30% in three months and driving 500 visits to her website per month. She chose her marketing channels based on where her target audience was most active: Instagram for visual content, a blog for SEO and content marketing, and an email newsletter for direct communication.

Emily created a content calendar that included daily Instagram posts featuring her candles in different settings, weekly blog articles on topics like candle care and home decor tips, and a monthly newsletter with product updates and special offers. She used high-quality photos and engaging captions to showcase her products and connect with her audience.

To boost her SEO, Emily researched relevant keywords and optimized her

CHAPTER 7: BUILDING YOUR BRAND AND MARKETING STRATEGY

website content. She also started a Pinterest account to drive traffic to her blog and website. For PPC advertising, she ran Google Ads targeting keywords like "eco-friendly candles" and "handmade candles."

Emily partnered with influencers in the home decor and lifestyle niches to reach a broader audience. She sent them free candles in exchange for honest reviews and social media posts. She also issued press releases to local media outlets and blogs to generate buzz about her new business.

By tracking her KPIs, Emily was able to see which marketing efforts were most effective. She noticed that her Instagram posts with behind-the-scenes content received higher engagement, so she started sharing more of her candle-making process. Her blog articles on home decor tips were driving significant traffic to her website, so she focused on creating more of that content.

Through consistent branding, a well-rounded marketing strategy, and careful analysis, Emily successfully built her handmade candle business. Her efforts paid off, and Cozy Glow became a popular brand among eco-conscious consumers and candle enthusiasts.

To wrap up, here are some key takeaways for building your brand and marketing strategy:

1. Define your brand identity with a memorable logo, colors, and fonts that reflect your business's essence.
   2. Develop a consistent brand voice that resonates with your target audience.
   3. Understand your target audience by creating detailed buyer personas.
   4. Set SMART marketing goals to stay focused and measure progress.
   5. Choose the marketing channels that best reach your target audience.
   6. Create a content calendar to plan and organize your marketing activities.
   7. Use analytics tools to track KPIs and make data-driven decisions.
   8. Continuously optimize your marketing strategy based on performance

data.

Building your brand and

marketing strategy is an ongoing process, but with a clear plan and a bit of creativity, you can attract and engage your target audience. So go ahead, let your brand shine, and watch your business grow.

Chapter 8: Setting Up Operations and Infrastructure

Alright, savvy entrepreneur, you've got your brand polished and your marketing strategy ready to roll. Now it's time to get into the nitty-gritty of setting up your operations and infrastructure. This chapter is all about laying the groundwork that will keep your business running smoothly day in and day out. Think of it as setting up the stage before the big show. You want everything in place, from the curtains to the lights, so you can focus on dazzling your audience with your performance.

First up, let's talk about choosing a location. Whether you're opening a brick-and-mortar store, setting up an office, or creating a home-based business, the location you choose can significantly impact your operations. If you're going the physical route, consider factors like foot traffic, accessibility, and proximity to suppliers and customers. A high-traffic area might cost more in rent, but it could also bring in more customers. On the other hand, if your business is primarily online, your focus will be more on your website and online presence, but you might still need a dedicated space for inventory and shipping.

For those opening a retail store, the layout and design of your space are crucial. You want to create an inviting environment that encourages customers to browse and buy. Think about the flow of your space—how customers will move through it, where you'll place your products, and how you'll use signage and displays. If you're opening a restaurant, consider the kitchen layout, dining area, and even the ambiance. The right setup can enhance the customer experience and streamline your operations.

Next, let's talk about equipment and technology. The tools you use can make a big difference in your efficiency and productivity. Start by identifying what you need to operate your business effectively. For a retail store, this might include point-of-sale (POS) systems, cash registers, barcode scanners, and security systems. For an office-based business, you'll need computers, printers, telephones, and perhaps specialized software.

Investing in the right technology can save you time and money in the long run. For example, a good POS system can help you manage inventory, track sales, and process payments quickly and accurately. Cloud-based software solutions can streamline your operations, allowing you to access data and manage your business from anywhere. Tools like Slack or Microsoft Teams can improve communication and collaboration within your team, especially if you're working remotely.

Now, let's move on to developing efficient operational processes and workflows. These are the routines and procedures that keep your business running smoothly. Start by mapping out your key processes, such as order fulfillment, inventory management, customer service, and accounting. Document each step and identify any bottlenecks or areas for improvement.

Standardizing your processes can help ensure consistency and quality. Create checklists, templates, and standard operating procedures (SOPs) for your team to follow. This not only makes training new employees easier but also ensures everyone is on the same page. For example, if you're running an e-commerce store, you might create SOPs for processing orders, handling returns, and managing customer inquiries.

CHAPTER 8: SETTING UP OPERATIONS AND INFRASTRUCTURE

Efficiency is the name of the game here. Look for ways to automate repetitive tasks. For instance, you can use software to automate your email marketing campaigns, schedule social media posts, or manage your inventory. Automation can free up your time to focus on more strategic tasks, like growing your business or developing new products.

Speaking of inventory management, this is a critical aspect of your operations, especially if you're selling physical products. You need to know what you have in stock, where it's located, and how much it's worth. An effective inventory management system helps you avoid stockouts, reduce excess inventory, and improve cash flow. Consider using inventory management software that integrates with your POS system and e-commerce platform. This will give you real-time visibility into your inventory levels and help you make informed decisions.

Customer service is another key component of your operations. Providing excellent customer service can set you apart from your competitors and build customer loyalty. Set up systems to handle customer inquiries, complaints, and feedback promptly and professionally. Train your team to deliver exceptional service, and consider using customer relationship management (CRM) software to track customer interactions and manage relationships. Happy customers are more likely to become repeat customers and refer others to your business.

Let's not forget about logistics and supply chain management. Whether you're sourcing raw materials, manufacturing products, or shipping orders to customers, a smooth supply chain is essential. Build strong relationships with your suppliers and have backup options in case of disruptions. If you're shipping products, consider your shipping options and choose reliable carriers. Offer tracking information to your customers to keep them informed about their orders.

Another important aspect of setting up your operations is establishing clear policies and procedures. This includes everything from your return policy to your employee handbook. Clearly defined policies help set expectations and provide guidelines for your team. They also protect your business by ensuring compliance with laws and regulations. Review your policies regularly and update them as needed to reflect changes in your business or industry.

Now, let's take a look at a real-life example. Meet Jason, who wants to start a specialty coffee shop. Here's how he set up his operations and infrastructure:

Jason began by choosing a prime location in a bustling downtown area with high foot traffic. He negotiated a lease for a cozy space with large windows and plenty of natural light. To create an inviting atmosphere, he invested in comfortable seating, stylish decor, and soft lighting. He designed the layout to ensure a smooth flow from the entrance to the counter, making it easy for customers to order and pick up their drinks.

Next, Jason focused on his equipment and technology needs. He purchased high-quality coffee machines, grinders, and brewing equipment. For his POS system, he chose a cloud-based solution that integrated with his inventory management and customer loyalty programs. This allowed him to track sales, manage inventory, and offer rewards to repeat customers seamlessly.

Jason developed efficient operational processes to ensure consistency and quality. He created detailed SOPs for everything from brewing coffee to cleaning the equipment. He also implemented a system for tracking inventory, ensuring he always had the right amount of coffee beans, milk, and other supplies on hand. To streamline his supply chain, Jason built strong relationships with local coffee roasters and suppliers, ensuring a steady supply of fresh, high-quality beans.

Customer service was a top priority for Jason. He trained his team to greet customers warmly, take orders accurately, and handle any issues promptly. He also set up a CRM system to track customer preferences and feedback, allowing

CHAPTER 8: SETTING UP OPERATIONS AND INFRASTRUCTURE

him to personalize the customer experience and address any concerns quickly.

Jason established clear policies and procedures for his business. He created an employee handbook outlining expectations, roles, and responsibilities. He also developed a return policy and guidelines for handling customer complaints. By setting clear expectations, Jason ensured his team knew what was expected of them and could deliver consistent service.

To handle logistics, Jason chose reliable shipping carriers for any online orders and offered tracking information to his customers. He also implemented a system for managing deliveries and restocking supplies, ensuring his coffee shop ran smoothly even during busy times.

By setting up efficient operations and infrastructure, Jason created a strong foundation for his specialty coffee shop. His attention to detail and focus on quality and customer service helped him build a loyal customer base and achieve success.

In conclusion, setting up your operations and infrastructure is a critical step in building a successful business. By choosing the right location, investing in the right equipment and technology, developing efficient processes, and providing excellent customer service, you can create a solid foundation for your business. Remember to continuously review and improve your operations to stay competitive and meet your customers' needs.

Here are some key takeaways for setting up your operations and infrastructure:

1. Choose a location that aligns with your business goals and target audience.
2. Invest in the right equipment and technology to improve efficiency and productivity.
3. Develop standardized processes and workflows to ensure consistency and quality.
4. Automate repetitive tasks to save time and focus on strategic activities.

5. Implement effective inventory management to avoid stockouts and reduce excess inventory.

6. Provide exceptional customer service to build loyalty and set yourself apart from competitors.

7. Establish clear policies and procedures to set expectations and ensure compliance.

8. Build strong relationships with suppliers and choose reliable shipping carriers for logistics.

9. Continuously review and improve your operations to stay competitive and meet customer needs.

By taking these steps, you'll set your business up for long-term success and be well-prepared to handle any challenges that come your way. So, roll up your sleeves, get your operations in order, and watch your business thrive.

Chapter 9: Hiring and Managing Your Team

Alright, you've laid the groundwork for your business, and now it's time to bring in some reinforcements. Hiring and managing a team can be one of the most rewarding yet challenging parts of running a business. Think of it like assembling your own superhero squad. You need a mix of talents, skills, and personalities to help your business soar to new heights. But remember, even superheroes need a good leader to guide them. So, let's dive into how to build and manage a stellar team.

First things first, let's talk about identifying your staffing needs. Start by assessing your business operations and determining what roles are essential for your success. Consider what tasks are taking up most of your time and where you could use some extra help. Do you need someone to handle customer service, manage your social media, or take care of administrative tasks? Make a list of the roles you need to fill and the skills required for each position.

Next, it's time to create job descriptions. A clear and detailed job description is crucial for attracting the right candidates. It should outline the responsibilities, qualifications, and expectations for the role. Be specific about the skills and experience you're looking for, but also include a bit about your company culture and what makes working for your business unique. You want to attract candidates who not only have the right skills but also fit well with your team.

Once you have your job descriptions ready, it's time to start the hiring process.

There are several ways to find potential candidates. You can post your job openings on popular job boards like Indeed, LinkedIn, or Glassdoor. You can also reach out to your network and ask for referrals. Sometimes, the best candidates come from personal recommendations. Don't underestimate the power of social media—posting about job openings on your business's social media channels can help you reach a wider audience.

When reviewing resumes and applications, look for candidates who not only meet the qualifications but also have a genuine interest in your business. A candidate who is passionate about your industry or shares your company values is likely to be a better fit and more motivated in their role. Once you've shortlisted candidates, it's time to conduct interviews. Prepare a mix of questions that assess both skills and cultural fit. For example, you can ask about their previous work experience, how they handle challenges, and why they're interested in working for your business.

During the interview process, it's important to create a positive candidate experience. Remember, the interview is a two-way street. Just as you're evaluating the candidate, they're also evaluating your business. Be professional, respectful, and transparent about the role and your expectations. Provide candidates with an opportunity to ask questions and learn more about your business. This not only helps them make an informed decision but also leaves a positive impression of your company.

Once you've found the right candidates, it's time to make an offer. Be clear about the terms of employment, including salary, benefits, and any other perks you're offering. Make sure to outline the job responsibilities and expectations again to ensure there's no confusion. When the candidate accepts your offer, it's time to move on to the onboarding process.

Onboarding is more than just filling out paperwork. It's about setting your new hires up for success and helping them feel welcome in your team. Start with a thorough orientation that covers your company's mission, values, and

CHAPTER 9: HIRING AND MANAGING YOUR TEAM

culture. Provide them with the tools and resources they need to do their job effectively. Introduce them to the team and set up a buddy system where an experienced team member can help them get acclimated.

Training is a crucial part of the onboarding process. Even if your new hires have the right skills, they still need to learn how things are done at your business. Provide comprehensive training that covers all aspects of their role, from the technical tasks to the company policies and procedures. Make sure to offer ongoing support and check in regularly to see how they're doing and if they need any additional help.

Managing your team effectively is key to maintaining a productive and positive work environment. Communication is the cornerstone of good management. Keep the lines of communication open and encourage your team to share their ideas, concerns, and feedback. Regular team meetings and one-on-one check-ins can help you stay connected with your team and address any issues before they become bigger problems.

Setting clear expectations and goals is also important. Make sure your team knows what's expected of them and how their work contributes to the overall success of the business. Use performance metrics to track progress and provide regular feedback. Recognize and reward good performance to motivate your team and show your appreciation for their hard work.

Creating a positive company culture is essential for keeping your team happy and engaged. Foster a culture of collaboration, respect, and inclusivity. Encourage teamwork and create opportunities for your team to bond and build relationships. This can be through team-building activities, social events, or simply creating a work environment where people feel comfortable and valued.

Let's look at a real-life example. Meet Rachel, who wants to start a boutique marketing agency. Here's how she built and managed her team:

Rachel began by identifying her staffing needs. She needed a mix of creative and technical talent, including graphic designers, copywriters, social media managers, and SEO specialists. She created detailed job descriptions for each role, outlining the responsibilities, qualifications, and what made working at her agency special.

Rachel posted the job openings on LinkedIn and asked for referrals from her network. She received a flood of applications and carefully reviewed each one, looking for candidates who not only had the right skills but also a passion for marketing and a good cultural fit. She conducted several rounds of interviews, asking a mix of technical questions and questions about their interest in the industry and how they handle challenges.

Once Rachel found her dream team, she made offers and welcomed them onboard with a comprehensive orientation and training program. She provided them with all the tools and resources they needed and introduced them to the rest of the team. Rachel created a buddy system, pairing new hires with experienced team members to help them get acclimated.

Rachel held regular team meetings to keep everyone in the loop and encourage open communication. She set clear expectations and goals for each team member and used performance metrics to track progress. She provided regular feedback and recognized and rewarded good performance.

To foster a positive company culture, Rachel encouraged teamwork and collaboration. She organized team-building activities, social events, and even created a comfortable and fun office environment with a cozy lounge area, snacks, and a ping-pong table. Her efforts paid off, and her team was happy, engaged, and productive.

In conclusion, hiring and managing a team is a critical part of running a successful business. By identifying your staffing needs, creating clear job descriptions, conducting thorough interviews, and providing comprehensive

CHAPTER 9: HIRING AND MANAGING YOUR TEAM

onboarding and training, you can build a strong and capable team. Effective management involves open communication, setting clear expectations, recognizing good performance, and fostering a positive company culture. With these strategies in place, you'll create a work environment where your team can thrive and contribute to the success of your business.

Here are some key takeaways for hiring and managing your team:

1. Identify your staffing needs and create clear job descriptions.
2. Use a mix of job boards, referrals, and social media to find potential candidates.
3. Conduct thorough interviews to assess skills and cultural fit.
4. Create a positive candidate experience and be transparent about the role and expectations.
5. Provide comprehensive onboarding and training to set new hires up for success.
6. Keep the lines of communication open and encourage feedback.
7. Set clear expectations and goals and use performance metrics to track progress.
8. Recognize and reward good performance to motivate your team.
9. Foster a positive company culture of collaboration, respect, and inclusivity.
10. Regularly review and improve your management practices to ensure your team remains happy and productive.

By focusing on these areas, you'll be well on your way to building and managing a team that will help your business reach new heights. So, put on your manager's hat, assemble your superhero squad, and lead them to success.

Chapter 10: Scaling and Growing Your Business

Alright, trailblazer, you've come a long way. You've got a solid business running, a dream team in place, and things are humming along nicely. Now, it's time to think about the next big step: scaling and growing your business. This is where you take everything you've built and expand it, reaching new markets, increasing your revenue, and maybe even becoming the next big thing. Scaling a business is an exciting yet challenging phase, and it requires careful planning and strategic execution. So, let's dive into how you can take your business to the next level.

First things first, what does it mean to scale your business? Simply put, scaling is about growing your business in a way that allows you to increase revenue without a corresponding increase in costs. It's about finding ways to do more with less, maximizing efficiency, and leveraging your existing resources. Scaling is not just about getting bigger; it's about getting smarter and more efficient.

To start, you need to have a clear growth strategy. This involves setting specific, measurable, achievable, relevant, and time-bound (SMART) goals for your business. Do you want to expand your product line, enter new markets, increase your online presence, or maybe open additional locations? Your growth strategy should align with your overall business goals and be based on

CHAPTER 10: SCALING AND GROWING YOUR BUSINESS

thorough market research and analysis.

One of the first steps in scaling your business is to ensure that your operations are efficient and scalable. This means having systems and processes in place that can handle increased demand without compromising quality. Take a close look at your current operations and identify any bottlenecks or inefficiencies. Can you streamline your production process, automate certain tasks, or outsource non-core activities? The goal is to create a scalable infrastructure that can support growth.

Next, consider your technology stack. Investing in the right technology can significantly enhance your efficiency and scalability. This might include upgrading your customer relationship management (CRM) system, implementing advanced analytics tools, or using cloud-based solutions to improve collaboration and data management. Technology can help you automate routine tasks, gain insights into your business performance, and provide a better experience for your customers.

Speaking of customers, they are the lifeblood of your business, and retaining them is crucial for sustainable growth. Focus on delivering exceptional customer service and building strong relationships with your customers. Happy customers are more likely to become repeat customers and refer others to your business. Consider implementing a loyalty program or offering incentives for referrals. Collect feedback regularly and use it to improve your products or services. Remember, word of mouth is a powerful marketing tool, and satisfied customers can be your best advocates.

Expanding your product or service offerings is another way to scale your business. Look for opportunities to diversify your product line or introduce new services that complement your existing offerings. This can help you reach new customer segments and increase your revenue streams. However, be careful not to overextend yourself. It's important to maintain the quality and integrity of your core products or services while exploring new opportunities.

Entering new markets is a significant step in scaling your business. This could mean expanding to new geographic regions, targeting different demographics, or even going international. Conduct thorough market research to understand the demand, competition, and cultural nuances of the new market. Adapt your marketing strategy and product offerings to meet the needs and preferences of the new audience. Establishing a strong local presence, either through partnerships or a dedicated team, can also help you succeed in new markets.

Now, let's talk about funding your growth. Scaling a business often requires additional capital to invest in new technology, hire more staff, increase marketing efforts, or expand operations. There are several ways to secure funding for your growth initiatives. You can reinvest profits, seek additional funding from investors, apply for business loans, or explore alternative financing options like crowdfunding. Whichever route you choose, it's important to have a clear plan for how you'll use the funds and how they'll contribute to your growth objectives.

Building a strong team is essential for scaling your business. As your business grows, you'll need more hands on deck to handle the increased workload and bring new ideas to the table. Hiring the right people and nurturing a positive company culture can make a significant difference in your ability to scale. Look for individuals who are not only skilled but also align with your company values and vision. Provide ongoing training and development opportunities to help your team grow alongside your business.

Effective leadership is crucial during the scaling phase. As the leader, you need to have a clear vision, communicate it effectively, and inspire your team to work towards common goals. Be open to feedback and willing to adapt your strategies as needed. Scaling a business comes with its share of challenges, and strong leadership can help you navigate the ups and downs.

Let's not forget about marketing. To scale your business, you need to reach a larger audience and attract more customers. This requires a robust marketing

CHAPTER 10: SCALING AND GROWING YOUR BUSINESS

strategy that leverages multiple channels and tactics. Consider investing in digital marketing, such as search engine optimization (SEO), pay-per-click (PPC) advertising, social media marketing, and email marketing. Content marketing can also be a powerful tool for building brand awareness and attracting new customers. Create valuable and relevant content that resonates with your target audience and showcases your expertise.

Partnerships and collaborations can also play a significant role in scaling your business. Look for strategic partnerships that can help you reach new customers, enhance your product offerings, or enter new markets. For example, partnering with complementary businesses can create cross-promotional opportunities and expand your reach. Collaborating with industry influencers or thought leaders can also help you build credibility and attract a wider audience.

Scaling a business is not without its challenges. As you grow, you may face issues like increased competition, operational complexities, and the need for more robust systems and processes. It's important to anticipate these challenges and have a plan in place to address them. Stay agile and be willing to adapt your strategies as needed. Regularly review your performance metrics and make data-driven decisions to stay on track.

To illustrate the process of scaling a business, let's look at a real-life example. Meet Sarah, who started a small artisanal soap business from her kitchen. After gaining a loyal customer base and positive reviews, Sarah decided it was time to scale her business. Here's how she did it:

Sarah began by setting clear growth goals. She wanted to increase her production capacity, expand her product line, and reach new markets. She started by streamlining her production process. Sarah invested in better equipment and automated some of the more time-consuming tasks. This allowed her to produce more soap without compromising quality.

Next, Sarah upgraded her technology stack. She implemented a more robust CRM system to manage customer relationships and track sales. She also started using advanced analytics tools to gain insights into customer behavior and preferences. This helped her make data-driven decisions and personalize her marketing efforts.

To retain her customers and attract new ones, Sarah focused on delivering exceptional customer service. She launched a loyalty program that rewarded repeat customers with discounts and exclusive offers. She also encouraged customers to leave reviews and share their experiences on social media.

Sarah expanded her product line by introducing new scents and product variations, such as bath bombs and body lotions. This helped her reach new customer segments and increase her revenue streams. She also started offering gift sets, which became popular during the holiday season.

Entering new markets was a significant step for Sarah. She began by targeting nearby cities and regions where there was demand for artisanal and eco-friendly products. She adapted her marketing strategy to resonate with the new audience and established partnerships with local boutiques to carry her products.

To fund her growth initiatives, Sarah reinvested her profits and sought additional funding from a small business loan. She used the funds to hire more staff, increase her marketing efforts, and expand her production facility. She also explored crowdfunding options to raise awareness and generate buzz for her new product launches.

Building a strong team was crucial for Sarah's success. She hired skilled individuals who were passionate about her mission and provided them with ongoing training and development opportunities. She also fostered a positive company culture that encouraged collaboration and innovation.

CHAPTER 10: SCALING AND GROWING YOUR BUSINESS

Effective leadership was key during the scaling phase. Sarah had a clear vision for her business and communicated it effectively to her team. She was open to feedback and willing to adapt her strategies as needed. Her strong leadership helped her navigate the challenges of scaling and stay focused on her goals.

Sarah invested in digital marketing to reach a larger audience. She optimized her website for SEO, ran targeted PPC campaigns, and created engaging content for her social media channels. She also collaborated with influencers in the beauty and wellness industry to increase her brand's visibility.

Partnerships played a significant role in Sarah's growth. She collaborated with complementary businesses, such as eco-friendly gift shops and wellness centers, to create cross-promotional opportunities. These partnerships helped her reach new customers and enhance her product offerings.

Scaling her business was not without challenges. Sarah faced increased competition, operational complexities, and the need for more robust systems and processes. However, she anticipated these challenges and had a plan in place to address them. She stayed agile and regularly reviewed her performance metrics to make data-driven decisions.

In conclusion, scaling and growing your business is an exciting and challenging phase that requires careful planning and strategic execution. By setting clear growth goals, streamlining your operations, investing in technology, retaining your customers, expanding your product offerings, entering new markets, securing funding, building a strong team, and leveraging marketing and partnerships, you can take your business to new heights. Stay agile, anticipate challenges, and be willing to adapt your strategies as needed. With the right approach, you can achieve sustainable growth and make your business a success. So, put on your growth hat, get ready to scale, and watch your business thrive.

Conclusion: Embracing the Entrepreneurial Journey

Congratulations, future business mogul! You've made it through the ten chapters of this guide, packed with insights, strategies, and real-life examples to help you navigate the thrilling yet challenging world of small business entrepreneurship. By now, you've got a solid foundation of knowledge and a toolkit full of practical tips to turn your dream into a successful reality. But before you go, let's wrap things up and revisit some key takeaways.

First and foremost, remember that entrepreneurship is a journey, not a destination. It's filled with twists and turns, highs and lows, and plenty of lessons along the way. The key is to stay resilient, adaptable, and passionate about your vision. You've got to be ready to embrace the unknown and take calculated risks. After all, it's the willingness to venture into uncharted territory that often leads to the most significant breakthroughs.

One of the most important steps in your journey is finding the right business idea. This involves looking at your passions, skills, and the market's needs. It's about identifying opportunities where you can make a meaningful impact and solve real problems. Your idea is the seed, but it's the research and validation that will help it grow into a thriving business.

Once you have your idea, conducting thorough market research is crucial.

CONCLUSION: EMBRACING THE ENTREPRENEURIAL JOURNEY

Understanding your target audience, competition, and industry trends will give you the insights needed to craft a business plan that stands out. This plan is your roadmap, guiding you through the startup phase and keeping you focused on your goals.

Securing funding and managing finances are next on the list. Whether you're bootstrapping, seeking investors, or applying for loans, having a clear financial strategy is essential. It's not just about getting the money; it's about managing it wisely to sustain and grow your business. Remember, cash flow is the lifeblood of your business.

The legal considerations and business structure you choose will set the framework for your operations. From selecting the right business entity to obtaining necessary licenses and protecting your intellectual property, getting these elements right from the start will save you headaches down the road.

Building your brand and marketing strategy is where you get to show off your creativity. Your brand is more than a logo; it's your business's personality and promise to your customers. A solid marketing strategy helps you reach your audience, engage them, and turn them into loyal customers.

Setting up efficient operations and infrastructure is all about creating systems that can handle growth. From the right location and equipment to technology and process optimization, these elements ensure your business runs smoothly and efficiently.

Hiring and managing a great team is critical. Your team is your biggest asset, and creating a positive, collaborative work environment will drive your business forward. Lead by example, communicate clearly, and foster a culture of innovation and respect.

Finally, scaling and growing your business is the exciting phase where you see all your hard work pay off. It's about expanding your reach, increasing your revenue, and continuously improving your operations. Keep an eye on the big picture, but don't forget to celebrate the small victories along the way.

In conclusion, starting and running a small business is no small feat, but it's incredibly rewarding. You've got the passion, the plan, and the perseverance to make it happen. Stay curious, keep learning, and don't be afraid to ask for help when you need it. Surround yourself with a supportive network of mentors, peers, and advisors who can offer guidance and encouragement.

So, here's to your entrepreneurial journey. May it be filled with innovation, growth, and success. Remember, the world needs your ideas, your creativity, and your determination. Now go out there and make your mark. You've got this!

Made in the USA
Monee, IL
17 November 2024